INTRODU TO PET FRIENDLY GARDENING

A comprehensive guide to gardening alongside pets including insider tips on how to start and maintain your first pet friendly garden, safe plants and many more

Emma Lucas

TABLE OF CONTENTS

INTRODUCTION

It's a common belief that a man's best friend is his pet. Well, as other devotees will confirm, they make terrific masters! A garden is essentially comparable in this regard. A garden provides our family with fresh vegetables, promotes neighborhood biodiversity, is calming and contemplative, and demands attention in exchange for maximizing these advantages. It makes sense that pets are welcome in our outside areas. Gardens should be accessible to all, and our furry friends are important parts of our families as well.

The two domains can sometimes seem to conflict for those who have a passion for both plants and animals. Pets shouldn't always be in gardens because many plants can be harmful to them. Dogs, cats, and other furry mammals dig up earth and uproot plants in playful curiosity. You need to understand the fundamentals of cultivating a garden that is pet-friendly if you spend a lot of time with your furry pals!

However, there is a way to combine these two worlds: which we refer to pet-friendly gardening. Although the phrase refers to a place that is "friendly" in the sense that it is not dangerous, I like to use it to refer to a place that is secure for your pets and created with their delight and play in mind.

Benefits of pet friendly gardening

Our relationship with nature has a direct impact on our well-being. This holds true for all living things without exception. A garden improves both physical and mental health, in addition to the many other evident advantages.

Any size organic garden can be a productive answer if we're seeking for ways to cut costs and minimize food waste. We don't need to buy fruits and vegetables from the store because we can grow them ourselves. Every salad matters, and some is better than none! Growing plants that are beneficial to our health and the health of our dogs, including edible flowers, herbs, and some types of grasses, is not difficult, but it does take some planning and attention. Certain plants can help keep pests away from the whole family.

Because a pet-friendly garden doesn't use fossil fuels for production, unlike certain commercial farms, it contributes to the reduction of carbon emissions. Grow your own edibles instead of consuming manufactured ones that are laced with toxins and frequently linked to environmental abuse and modern slavery! Planting a small amount of catnip, mint, or medicinal violets in a somewhat shaded nook can be a simple solution. Pretty potent & guilt free.

CHAPTER ONE

Establishing a safe Garden Space

Have you ever considered your garden to be more than a collection of plants? By "safe garden," we mean that you should choose plants that won't injure your pets. This book will assist you in selecting plants that will keep your fur balls healthy because some plants may appear nice but may not be good for them. It's similar to designating a secure area in your garden for your pets to hang around.

However, it's not just about safety, it's also about bringing life and positivity to your garden. Imagine your pets lounging in the shade, exploring the area, or sniffing flowers. We're looking at how dogs and plants can work together to create a lively, buzzing garden.

Furthermore, gardening is therapeutic for both you and your dogs and is about more than simply lovely flowers. Your yard turns into this enchanted space where your pets can play, explore, or just relax in the company of nature.

We're going to talk about how you arrange your garden in addition to plant selections. Consider it as setting up distinct spaces for your pets, such as a play area or a peaceful area where they may relax. It all comes down to ensuring sure your pets are comfortable in your outdoor area.

This section serves as the beginning of everything else in the book. It all comes down to making your garden a fun, secure, and extremely pet-friendly area. So, let's get set to change your outdoor area into a warm haven for both plants and pets.

What should I look for in plants for my pet-friendly gardening

Look for poisonous plants. If our pets consume some plants, they may become poisonous. Steer clear of any hazardous or poisonous ones! These include flowering plants like azaleas, daffodils, chrysanthemums, and rhododendrons, as well as mushrooms like Amanita phalloides [death cap].

Plants with tough texture should be used. If a cat or dog enjoys chewing on objects [and who doesn't?], then it's better to stay away from using any plants with slender stems and leaves since they'll probably get devoured rapidly. Rather, choose types with stronger leaves, like lavender or rosemary, as they will withstand those pointed teeth!

In particular, individuals who have children and dogs should avoid using pesticides in their gardens as they are more likely to come into contact with harmful substances. Not all "pests" are killed by pesticides. They are toxic to all living things.

How to Design a Garden That Is Pet-Friendly

You can design a garden that is not only safe for your pets to wander in, but also tailored to meet their needs, if you have a little additional backyard space. Here are some pointers to get your pet-friendly garden started.

Use these suggestions if you have a section of your backyard that you are prepared to set aside for your dogs. Depending on how big your space is and the pets you have, some of them might not apply to you. However, they will provide you with some ideas to help you design the ideal pet-friendly area.

Select Secure Plants

Before all other considerations, safety is the most crucial element of a pet-friendly landscape. It is essential to choose plants that are safe for your pets to handle and won't hurt them in any way, even if they nibble on them or are touched by them.

Many plants are safe to eat, however others can be fatal if consumed in high quantities or dangerous if ingested. It's imperative that you keep these out of any area you plan to dedicate for your pet.

Local veterinary information (or chatting to your vet personally) will help you select what plants are appropriate for a pet-friendly setting. Depending on the kind of pets you have, there are also pet-friendly seed collections with a wide range of choices suitable for animals. Also in the later part of the book we will be discussing on some of the plants that are toxic and the ones that are beneficial to our pets.

<u>Make Room for Play</u>

Create play areas in your outside pet habitats to encourage interaction, exercise, and the avoidance of interior trouble. Ample space is necessary for many pets, especially dogs, to run around and play. If you're lucky, they might be able to amuse themselves inside your home. Sadly, the majority of houses don't, which is why pet-friendly gardens are important.

While planning the location, make sure you reserve some space for play. This may be a designated sand hole for excitable digging, an obstacle course with a few tempting snacks along the way, or just an open area of lawn for running around. Since you are the one who knows your dogs the best, use that expertise to build a play space that they will adore.

There's more benefit attached to this tip. Your dogs are less likely to cause trouble in areas of your garden or house that you don't want them to when they are worn out from playing in their incredibly exciting garden space. Their day will be filled with targeted stimulation, which will also provide them some much-needed exercise as they run around.

Choose Plants Your Pets Will Appreciate

When you are collecting plants, your primary concern will be safety. Beyond that, though, you may also select secure plants that your pets will like playing with.

If you have cats, this suggestion is straightforward. Cats are particularly fond of a few plants, the name of which conveniently includes the word "cat" to signify the relationship. Cat grass is well-known for being an excellent indoor digestive help. Another well-liked choice that is quite simple to produce and can keep your cat busy for hours is catnip.

Dogs, especially the ones who adore rewards, are frequently lot less picky. Dogs can eat a wide variety of greens, flowers, and vegetables including corn and squash.

Some puppies adore cucumbers and relish biting into fresh slices during the sweltering summer months. Before you plant any vegetables in the garden, observe which ones your dog's enjoy.

For all other pets, the same holds true. Discovering their passions will help you include them in your pet-friendly gardening.

<u>Maintain Your Fences</u>

In addition to delineating the limits of our landscape, fences are essential for keeping our pets safe inside and outside of potential danger zones. However, just like any other garden feature, fences can sustain damage that reduces its usefulness.

Frequent fluctuations in the weather, moisture, and even our pets themselves can wear down a fence's structure and create possible weak points. To stop unforeseen escapes, it's critical to keep an eye out for these openings and close them.

Additionally, a well-kept fence will improve your garden's overall appearance. A damaged or worn-out fence definitely appears unkempt and takes away from the allure of your well-kept backyard that is pet-friendly.

Regularly go around the edge of your garden to look for evidence of wear or damage. Check for any sections that appear to be mostly worn out, loose boards, or rusting metal. You may also find these locations by keeping an eye on your pets outside; they'll probably discover them far sooner than you do.

As soon as you become aware of any problems, make sure to resolve them. Small openings may not look like much, but they can serve as inviting escape routes for inquisitive animals or points of entry for unwanted species. You may play with your pets in comfort knowing that your backyard is secure if you provide regular upkeep and prompt repairs.

Keep an eye on your pet's outside

Seeing your pets explore the garden can give you important information on how to design a pet-friendly space.

Observe them closely to find out what places they like to hang out, what plants they are drawn to, and which regions they frequent. Afterwards, you may use this information to create a pet-friendly garden that considers their preferred locations and plants while avoiding areas that might not be used or harmed.

Use the routine your pets currently have in your backyard to your advantage and create an even more fascinating area they will enjoy.

Protect Your Precious Plants

You most likely have certain plants in your garden that you really cherish. It is a good idea to keep these priceless plants out of the reach of energetic pets and in protected settings, whether or not they are safe.

They could gnaw on the leaves or blossoms, excavate around the roots, scuff the plants, or even run right through them, uprooting the whole thing. That's the last thing you want if you've worked hard to grow and tend to your priceless ornamental or food plants.

To ensure their safety, keep these plants segregated from the remainder of your garden that is suitable for pets. Fences and other plants, such as dense hedging, can be used as long as they are secure and prevent access by your four-legged pals.

Raised beds that are tall are another technique to keep particular plants safe. Smaller pets may be unable to access plants and soil with this method, but it might not be effective for agile cats or large dogs.

Incorporate Shelter

You need to think about shelter if you want your pets to spend the most of the day outside in their pet-friendly area. Pets shouldn't spend their entire day in the sun, just like people shouldn't. To keep your dogs safe and happy, you must give them shelter from the elements during the day.

Any overhead covering helps to offer protection from the sun and rain. You can designate an area for lounging outside with pergolas covered in vines that are suitable for pets, awnings fastened to the side of your house, or even shade sails. Throughout the day, take into account the direction of the sun to make sure the areas are shaded during the hottest times of the day, which are from midday to early afternoon.

You can add screens to lessen the effects of strong winds or create covered areas away from chilly temperatures close to your house to make the area more comfortable. Your house can act as a shelter for pets that are indoors most of the day and have easy access to the outside world. However, for people who spend the most of their day outside, this advice is crucial.

Shut Off Visible Soil

To stop pets from digging, hide exposed dirt areas with ground cover plants or pet-safe mulch.

Dogs and cats alike enjoy playing in the dirt. Regretfully, this causes certain ugly spots to remain throughout your garden, giving it an unkempt appearance. You still want your backyard to appear nice without the odd crater ruining your view, even if you do provide area for your pets.

Pets find open patches of dirt to be quite alluring. It's advisable to cover any exposed areas with pet-safe mulch or garden ground cover to discourage them from digging. As many people with pups and lawns already know, this may not put an end to them entirely. However, it will obscure the view and create a barrier that can divert attention from the excavation work.

Not only does this eliminate ugly holes from your garden, but it also makes your landscape seem better overall. Even with just a few ground cover seeds, your garden will look more lush and well-planned if you cover the empty land with foliage. Groundcover plants can reduce the amount of time you need to mow your grass and increase backyard biodiversity.

Reduce the Use of Hazardous Chemicals

In order to care for our plants and shield them from harmful pests and illnesses, we frequently reach for fertilizers, insecticides, and herbicides in the garden when we run into issues. But when it comes to cultivating a pet-friendly garden, these easy fixes aren't secure.

Particularly when consumed, several garden chemicals can seriously endanger an animal's health. Depending on the type of chemicals employed, there are a variety of problems to watch out for, from stomach problems to skin irritations.

Reducing the use of chemicals doesn't have to mean sacrificing care. You may preserve the health of the garden without endangering your pet's safety by using compost, natural predators, and environmentally suitable substitutes instead of dangerous chemicals. Additionally, this lessens harm to other local fauna, such as beneficial pollinators and birds that we wish to have in our gardens.

Before introducing any new product into your yard, always make sure you read the labels and know what's in them. If you're unsure, ask your veterinarian or search for pet-friendly certifications to be sure it's totally safe.

Store Instruments in the Shed

A well-kept garden often needs a variety of equipment, such as trowels, shears, and spades. Although they are essentials, they might be dangerous to inquisitive pets. If left in a location where your pets could try to play with them, sharp edges and pointy ends might cause serious mishaps.

The ideal answer is a shed or storage room, which keeps the tools orderly and out of the reach of curious pets. When tending a garden that is pet-friendly, establish a routine for putting away your tools after use.

This preserves and extends the life of your instruments in addition to protecting your pets. Although garden tools are built to last, proper storage is required when not in use. Your tools will stay rust-free and usable if they are kept out of the weather in a garage or shed.

<u>Keep Your Pool Covered</u>

Pets are protected from accidents and are kept from consuming chlorinated water by pool covers.

Pools are a great addition to landscapes because of their practicality and style. It's difficult to argue against the slick vibe that a well-designed pool offers while providing a lovely escape from the scorching summer heat.

Unfortunately, when cultivating a pet-friendly garden, pools present a risk. All they need to fall in at ground level is a straightforward accident. Fortunately, a lot of pets will be able to swim to safety. However, an unsupervised pool poses a major risk if your pet is not accustomed to swimming or if it is impossible to escape from your pool.

Large volumes of chlorinated pool water are also unsafe to ingest. Even if freshwater access is provided, a neglected swimming pool could attract hydration-seeking animals.

Covering your pool when it's not in use will address both issues. This method keeps dirt and debris out of the pool and helps maintain regular pool temperatures, which makes it useful in any garden, not just ones with pets.

Safety Points to Remember

Toxic plants

By selecting harmless plants, you can prevent unintentional poisoning of your pet. Many common garden plants, such as azaleas, rhododendrons, yew, autumn crocus, and English ivy, are harmful to dogs and/or cats. Daffodil and tulip bulbs are not good for dogs or cats to play with. Lilies are harmful to cats. Additionally, keep in mind that many of the species that can grow wild in your garden, including mushrooms which are poisonous. As another illustration, the toxic weed white snakeroot (Ageratina altissima) is toxic to all animals when consumed. Snakeroot should be removed and disposed of right away, just like mushrooms.

Plants with thorns

Keep an eye out for any thorns in the pet's soft foot pads and keep an eye out for any scratches that can go serious. Your dog may sustain eye injuries if they run headlong into a rose. Loss of eyesight and long-term damage could result from even a small cut or accident.

Fertilizers and pesticides

Use and store pesticides and fertilizers appropriately. Keep them in safe, clearly marked containers. Before using anything, make sure you carefully read the label.

When more friendly pesticide is not available, after using chemicals, keep your pets out of the garden for the specified period of time. Pet friendly alternatives include:

- Fertilizing with worm castings or fish fertilizer
- Removing aphids and spider mites with a powerful spray of water or with an application of horticultural oil.
- It seems that pulling and hoeing weeds lessens the demand for herbicides.

Ticks, mosquitoes, and fleas.

Ticks and other dangerous insects may be found in tall grasses. By clearing off leaf litter and cutting and pruning turf grass, you can contribute to their population decline. Check for mosquitoes once a week by clearing away any standing water and changing the water in birdbaths.

Compost

To prevent your pets from eating the contents, secure your compost bin. Consuming stale veggies might be highly hazardous.

Mulch

As gardeners, we understand the importance of mulch in keeping weeds under control and aiding in water retention. However, keep in mind that cocoa mulch contains the same component that makes chocolate poisonous to dogs. Pick natural wood chips like pine or cedar instead. Color-dyed wood mulches may cause allergic reactions in your pet.

Petscaping

Consider trying petscaping if you adore both your gardens and your pets. The purpose of this kind of garden design is to protect your furry friends without letting them ruin your lovely yard. Use these ideas to design areas that are pet-friendly.

If you make every decision with your pet's safety in mind, your petscaping design will turn out well. Setting borders, offering shade, granting access to fresh water, and incorporating sites for disposal are all components of the design. You must include areas for your dog to run and play if you own one.

Define limits

It's important that your dog learns to heed simple commands, even when you might not be able to train your cat. Dogs can discern which parts of the yard are forbidden. To indicate the boundaries, use short fences or borders. Your dog will be able to distinguish limits if all of the barriers are made of the same material. Planting spaces with raised beds may act as a deterrent. If you erect perimeter fencing and your pet enjoys patrolling the area, you should leave the planting beds and the fence two or three feet apart.

Make regions that are heavily planted

Tender plants are protected by dense plantings. Use robust perennials and hardy shrubs to provide protection for vulnerable plants.

Make space available for exercising

Canines are meant to run. Give your dog space to run around and play in the grassy area of your yard. If you allow your pet a special space to exercise, they'll be less inclined to bolt through your beds. Offer playthings like a ball knot toy suspended from a bungee cable.

Create routes

Pathways can assist in teaching your pet where it is appropriate and inappropriate to be in the garden. Making a pathway out of the path your pet typically travels to a favorite spot is a great way to address this issue. Don't use anything pointy; instead, choose paw-friendly surfaces like flagstones or flat gravel.

Construct a dig site

Dogs dig, so give them access to a dig pit so they may indulge in their innate curiosity. Put sand in the pit. Stuff toys, bones, or candies slightly below the surface. Congratulate your pet for digging in the designated spot.

Establish a zone for removal

Make an area specifically for your dog to relieve itself to avoid ugly dark streaks on the lawn that are caused by nitrogen in dog urine. Teach your dog to utilize this space. Installing a motion-activated sprayer or covering the soil with unpleasant materials like chicken wire will discourage cats from urinating in your flower beds. Construct a sandbox for cats. Nepeta cataria, or catnip plants, can be placed all around the litterbox to draw in your pet.

Offer water and shade

Dogs are particularly vulnerable to heat because they have few sweat glands. Make sure you have enough sun protection. Maintaining your pet's hydration is equally crucial, so have some fresh water on hand.

Sketching Your Strategy

Draft a garden plan at scale. Place a piece of tracing paper on top and draw the sun's and the shadows' locations. Show your dog the routes he or she takes around the property; these will eventually become your designated routes. Put in the particulars that suit your pet's demands, such a digging trench, and mark any spots that are of special importance. Include plants, especially any that are edible to animals, such as valerian, lemon grass, and catnip for cats, and additional fruit and vegetables for dogs. If you are planning to alter your pet's diet, don't forget to consult your veterinarian.

Selecting pet-friendly plants is just one aspect of petscaping. It opens the prospect of owning outdoor pets and a beautiful garden. A lovely area made possible by petscaping allows you and your animal friends to live and play in safety.

CHAPTER TWO

Top Houseplants for Pets

One of the best ways to lighten up your living area is to add some greenery to your house. But if you have a pet, you might be reluctant to introduce plants into your house because of worries about their toxicity.

Houseplants that are safe for your pets are a wonderful way to liven up your space without endangering your animals. They may bring a little greenery into any space, lessen tension, and enhance air quality.

Large dogs can benefit from owning a variety of pet-friendly houseplants, such as palm trees, banana plants, and olive trees. These larger plants are suitable for your pet buddies and may lend a dramatic touch to any space.

Pets can safely handle a variety of succulents, such as echeveria and string of pearls. To make sure succulents are safe for your dogs, it's crucial to do your homework before bringing any into your house.

Popular pet-friendly houseplants are listed below:

<u>Watermelon Plant or Aluminum Plant</u>

The aluminum plant, which belongs to the genus Pilea, is a visually pleasing and non-toxic plant for dogs and cats because of its variegated gray-and-green leaves. It grows well in medium to low light, stays less than 12 inches long, and only requires water when the top inch of soil becomes dry. You can grow it practically anywhere that's out of reach of your animal pals because it can withstand low light.

Friendship Plant

The friendship plant, which is closely linked to the aluminum plant, gets its name from how simple it is to split and share. In the event that you receive one as a present, you may be confident that dogs and cats cannot harm this plant, even if they manage to nibble on its fuzzy, crinkly leaves. Friendship plants thrive best in terrariums with high humidity levels, can withstand medium and low light levels, and often don't go much taller than 12 inches.

Calathea

Calathea plants are recognized for their vivid, patterned leaves. Since they are safe for both dogs and cats, they are a great option for pet owners. Calathea is well recognized for its ability to purify the air and has beautiful markings on its leaves resembling fishbones. Because it requires some shade, this houseplant is ideal for a plant stand or shelf in a bedroom with little natural light.

Orchid

Houseplants that are great for pets to have include orchids like the Phalaenopsis. They are a safe addition to homes with furry friends because they are not poisonous to cats or dogs. Their magnificent, enduring blossoms imbue any area with grace and serenity. Orchids are aesthetically pleasing and safe, making them a great addition to any pet owner's home where people and animals coexist in harmony.

Praying Plant

A popular houseplant for pets, the prayer plant is recognized for its eye-catching variegated foliage and vivid patterns. Its habit of folding its leaves at night to resemble praying hands gave it its name. Due to its non-toxic properties, it is a great option for pet owners and adds both style and safety to any home.

Spider Plant

Because the spider plant is non-toxic, both cats and dogs can safely keep it as a houseplant. Its ability to filter the air gets rid of dangerous pollutants, making indoor spaces healthier. It's a great option for busy pet owners because of its robustness and low maintenance requirements. The spider plant enhances the visual appeal and usability of any pet-friendly house with its distinctively curved leaves and low maintenance requirements.

Venus Flytraps

A popular houseplant for pets, the Venus flytrap is named for its enticing hinged traps that close in response to insects. It is a natural and environmentally friendly pest control option for homes because of its exceptional capacity to capture and break down little pests. Because of its fascinating qualities and non-toxic makeup, pet owners should give it some thought in order to protect their furry friends.

Boston Fern

The Boston Fern is a pet-friendly houseplant that is well-known for its vibrant green foliage. Its ability to filter the air makes it unique and improves the quality of indoor air. It is non-toxic to dogs and cats, making it a safe and attractive houseplant that also fosters a healthy living environment for people. For these reasons, pet owners should choose it as a houseplant.

Banana Plant

Pet-friendly houseplants, such as the Musa Dwarf Cavendish banana plant, are a great choice. Their thick, luscious leaves give your house a touch of the tropics and are safe for both dogs and cats to play with. They are an excellent option for pet owners because to their durability and air-purifying properties, which also make them a visually appealing and safe green addition to any living area.

The Money Tree

Dogs and cats cannot harm the money tree plant, making it a pet-friendly houseplant. It is a beautiful addition to any home because of its unusual braided trunk and thick green leaves. Pet owners may safely appreciate its visual appeal and incorporate a little bit of nature into their living environment without having to worry about endangering their furry friends.

Indoor Palm Trees

Because they are non-toxic, indoor palms like the Dypsis Areca are suitable houseplants for pets. Their air-purifying properties encourage a healthier living environment while their lush, tropical appearance lends an aura of luxury to any space. These palms are aesthetically pleasing, safe for curious animals, and an excellent way to purify the air in houses, so pet owners should give them some thought.

Parlor Palm

A parlor palm might be a good choice for pet owners who want to bring a little tree inside. This low-maintenance, non-toxic plant is a great place for novices to start, as it works well for both dogs and cats. Although it can withstand low light, it thrives best in bright, indirect light. Water your parlor palm when the top inch of soil becomes dry; it can grow up to eight feet, while four feet is the average height.

Christmas Cactus

One pet-friendly houseplant that is well-known for its colorful flowers throughout the holiday season is the Christmas cactus (Schlumbergera). It is a safe option for houses with dogs and cats because of its non-toxic nature. This unique plant is a great option for pet owners because it brings a festive touch to your home, requires little upkeep, and improves the health of both humans and pets.

Few Types of Ferns

Since many plants bearing the word "fern" in their names don't truly belong to the fern family, identifying ferns can be difficult. True ferns, such maidenhair and Boston ferns, are acceptable choices for pet-safe indoor plants. But watch out for poisonous misnomers, such as asparagus fern, which belongs to the lily family. The majority of ferns have similar requirements, despite differences in size: they enjoy high humidity, equally moist soil, and indirect sun.

Few Herbs

Growing herbs indoors is a simple way to infuse home-cooked meals with new flavors. But when it comes to the safety of pets, not all herbs are made equal. Conventional favorites like lavender and oregano are not pet-friendly, but houseplants like thyme, basil, and sage are. After the top inch of soil dries out, water your herbs and place them in a window that receives at least four or five hours of direct sunlight each day.

Vegetables and fruits

If your dog eats grapes, raisins, or mushrooms, it could cause serious stomach problems and kidney damage. These foods are quite dangerous for dogs. Persin, a toxin found in avocado skin, pits, and leaves, makes dogs throw up and have diarrhea. Although dogs love onions and garlic, these foods can be quite harmful. Ingesting them may result in diarrhea, vomiting, and—most importantly—rupturing your dog's red blood cells. Dogs can safely consume red tomatoes, however, solanine, a toxin found in green, unripe tomatoes, will make them sick. Pick your produce carefully because many fruits and veggies are good for us but bad for our dogs.

Some fruits and vegetables that are suitable for pets include:

- Squashed butternuts
- Carrots
- Cucumbers
- Berries
- Carrots
- Apples
- Watermelon
- Zucchini
- Spinach
- Celery
- Peas & Beans
- Ripe Tomatoes
- Cooked potatoes (if you want to share potatoes with your dog)

Since watermelon is nearly entirely composed of water, it's a great method to keep your dog hydrated on hot summer days. Berries are very high in fiber and packed with vitamins and antioxidants, so your dog will enjoy them! To give them a refreshing summer treat, you can freeze them or mash them into a paste and store in the refrigerator.

Due to their anti-inflammatory qualities, raspberries are excellent for aging dogs' joints. But they also contain trace levels of xylitol. The pancreas of your dog will mistake this sugar replacement for real sugar and secrete insulin to store it, which may weaken them and perhaps cause seizures. Therefore, give your dog no more than a cup of raspberries on any given occasion. Green beans and spinach are full in iron and vitamins, but they are also high in oxalic acid, which blocks the body's capacity to absorb calcium if eaten in large amounts and can contribute to renal problems.

Plants that are Harmful to Dogs & Cats

Do your homework before purchasing houseplants to ensure that they are safe for your four-legged pals as well as for the growing environment. Here are a few to stay away from:

Sago Palm

The sago palm (Cycas revoluta), grown for its eye-catching fronds and carefree disposition, is actually a cycad. The plant, albeit attractive in appearance, is exceedingly dangerous if pets eat any part of it, with the seeds being the most lethal. Cycasin is the poisonous principle; symptoms include internal hemorrhaging, jaundice, liver failure, drooling, vomiting, bloody feces, and fluid retention in the abdomen area. Due to the severity and seriousness of the symptoms, prompt medical attention is required.

Plant Jade

The jade plant (Crassula ovata), a succulent that was first brought to homes decades ago, is prized for its succulent leaves, which are thick and resemble robust trees, giving it an air of exoticism. If any portion of the plant is consumed by dogs or cats, it is harmful; the plant's poisonous nature is unclear. The usually moderate symptoms include depression, tiredness, loss of appetite, vomiting, and, in severe cases, a slowed heartbeat or convulsions.

Begonia

Begonia (Begonia spp.) is a popular houseplant and garden plant that is grown for its colorful flowers and eye-catching heart-shaped leaves that come in an array of colors and patterns. The toxic principle, soluble calcium oxalates, which are more abundant in the subterranean tubers than the leaves and stems, is poisonous to cats and dogs if consumed. Vomiting, diarrhea, mouth soreness, dehydration, difficulty swallowing, loss of appetite, and excessive salivation are among the usually mild side effects.

Zamioculcas Zamiifolia

The ZZ plant (Zamioculcas zamiifolia), whose name has been shortened for convenience by the nursery trade, is one of the hardest-working and most tolerant houseplants. The lustrous meaty leaves and graceful arching habit hold up well in low light and even flourish on neglect, making this a superb choice for those with hectic schedules. If pets consume calcium oxalate, it has a mild to moderately hazardous effect that might result in swelling of the skin, mucous membranes, or eyes. Most of the time, the symptoms of diarrhea, vomiting, and stomach aches should go away on their own.

Amaryllis

An enormous amaryllis bulb (Hippeastrum) develops a tall, sturdy stem with massive, trumpet-shaped flowers that come in a range of hues, making it a favorite among those who offer Christmas gifts. Belladonna lily, St. Joseph lily, cape belladonna, and naked lady are some more frequent names. Lycorine which is found in in amaryllis is toxic that is mildly to moderately dangerous to dogs and cats. It can produce tremors, depression, diarrhea, vomiting, abdominal pain, hypotension, and excessive salivation. Compared to the leaves and flowers, the bulbs are more poisonous.

Aloe Vera

Aloe (Aloe Vera) is a succulent that grows naturally in tropical places all over the world and is well-known for its numerous medicinal purposes. Cultivated for its spiky architectural form and ease of maintenance, aloe Vera can be cultivated indoors or outdoors in warm regions. The main application for the leaf gel is as a topically applied burn salve. Aloe Vera is internally used for a variety of various medical conditions. Saponin, a toxin found in aloe species, has foaming qualities akin to soap and can be harmful to dogs if consumed. Vomiting, diarrhea, fatigue, color changes in the urine, and (in rare cases) tremors are among the symptoms. Most of the time, toxicity is mild to moderate, but in rare circumstances, consumption may be fatal due to the potential for severe dehydration.

Dumb Cane

With its white and green variegated leaves, dumb cane (Dieffenbachia) adds a lush, tropical appeal to any room without requiring a lot of maintenance. Known by another name, leopard lily, it is one of the most popular houseplants. Despite its beauty, the plant contains harmful enzymes and oxalate crystals that burn pets' mouths when they eat on the leaves or stems. Drooling, vomiting, oral pain, decreased appetite, and (very infrequently) trouble breathing or swallowing are among the mild to moderate symptoms.

Snake Vine

Snake plant (Sansevieria trifasciata) is an almost indestructible houseplant that gives dramatic appeal to any space. It is grown for its spear-like variegated leaves and erect appearance. This African tropical, sometimes called mother-in-law's tongue, good luck plant, or viper's bowstring hemp, likes bright indirect light and little moisture. The hazardous principle, saponin, exhibits foaming qualities comparable to those of soap and is poisonous if consumed by dogs. Typically mild to moderate in nature, symptoms include drooling, nausea, vomiting, and diarrhea.

Fig

Weeping fig (Ficus benjamina), a widely grown tree native to Asia and Australia, is planted outside in warmer parts of the United States. It is planted as a houseplant because of its glossy leaves, attractive arching habit, and ability to withstand a variety of growth environments. Benjamin's fig, Indian rubber plant, and rubber tree are some more common names. All portions of the plant include the enzyme ficin, which is toxic to cats and dogs alike and can damage proteins in dogs that are essential for tissue healing. Fucisin, the other hazardous material, can irritate skin when exposed to sunlight and cause photosensitivity. Agitation, diarrhea, drooling, appetite loss, mouth pain, and vomiting are some of the symptoms. Blisters, inflammation, and redness are examples of skin symptoms. Generally speaking, toxicity is low unless greater doses are consumed.

Philodendron

Because philodendrons can tolerate a wide range of growth circumstances, especially low light, they have been a staple plant among houseplant enthusiasts for years. Preferred for its ornamental leaves and creeping habit, the heartleaf philodendron (Philodendron scandens), the most often cultivated variety, is also one of the easiest houseplants to maintain. Often called the "sweetheart plant," if chewed or consumed by cats or dogs, the leaves may be poisonous. Chewing or biting any portion of the plant releases the calcium oxalate crystals' poisonous component. Drooling, mouth soreness and swelling, decreased appetite, vomiting, and (in rare cases) narrowing of the airways are some of the symptoms. Most of the time, toxicity is low to moderate.

Calla Lily

The exquisite tubular blossoms of the calla lily (Zantedeschia aethiopica), which may be grown both indoors and outdoors, are its most notable feature. Calcium oxalate crystals are the plant's main toxicity, therefore pets should not consume any portions of the plant. Less severe symptoms include drooling, trouble swallowing, choking, and a burning sensation in the mouth and throat, which can last for up to two weeks. When significant amounts are consumed infrequently, symptoms might include mortality, seizures, vomiting, breathing problems, renal failure, and irreversible liver or kidney damage. Usually, there is mild to severe toxicity.

Kalanchoe

Grown for its colorful flowers and pretty scalloped leaves, kalanchoe (Kalanchoe blossfeldiana) is a staple of florist shops and garden stores. Houseplant enthusiasts enjoy this tropical succulent since it's easy to grow and can withstand a lot of different situations. The names "flaming Katy," "devil's backbone," "Mexican hat plant," and "Malawi's thrill" are also frequently used. Dogs and cats should not handle this plant in any way since it contains glycoside toxins, which are also dangerous. These toxins are similar to those found in foxglove. The majority of the time, poisoning is mild to moderate, and symptoms include diarrhea, vomiting, and drooling. Seizures, tremors, dilated pupils, irregular heart rate, and lethargy are possible extreme effects.

How to prevent your pets from getting near your houseplants

Keep your plants out of reach

Plant stands and hanging planters will make it more difficult for your pets to get to your plants.

Put off with a stench

Certain scents, such those of lavender, lemon, and garlic, can repel your pets. Your pets will turn away from your greenery if you mix them into the water and spritz your plants. In all that you do, avoid using vinegar! Some think that diluting vinegar with water is a remedy, but in reality, it does more harm than good to leaves.

Covering exposed soil

Use big boulders to cover the dirt if your pet enjoys digging and scratching at your plants. This covers up the loose dirt that initially drew them in.

Select plants especially for your animals

Provide your pets with a more appetizing chew toy to divert their interest away from your plants. Plants that are safe to eat and satisfy your pet's need to consume plants include basil, chamomile, thyme, and mint.

You can employ deterrents, such as bitter sprays or putting plants out of reach, to prevent pets from eating plants. To keep your pets busy and deter them from nibbling on leaves, you may also provide them an abundance of toys and goodies.

What can I do if my pet ingest poison

If dog owners think their dog has been poisoned, they should call their veterinarian right away or visit the closest vet clinic.

Keeping your cat and dog secure outside

Better weather, longer days, and perhaps more time spent in the garden with your pet are all signs of spring. You should be aware of some of the poisons and equipment that could endanger your pet, whether you intend to resume gardening or you're just going to be outside more.

Wasp and bee stings in cats and dogs

As the weather warms, wasps and bees begin to resurface, and your pet is very likely to get stung at some point in their lives. Dogs, because of their playful and curious temperament, are the most common pets to suffer from wasp and bee stings. Most of the time, a sting will only result in little discomfort, so you might not even need to see your veterinarian. Avoid using tweezers to extract the sting as this may extract additional venom. Instead, carefully scrape the stinger off with a stiff piece of card. To lessen swelling and pain, wrap an ice pack in a towel and apply it to the affected area.

On the other hand, many stings within the mouth or throat might be dangerous and necessitate an urgent visit to the veterinarian. The chemicals in the sting may also cause them to experience a significant allergic reaction.

The following are signs of a pet's allergic reaction to wasp and bee stings:

- All-around weakness
- Having trouble breathing
- Severe swelling

As the swelling may obstruct the airway, call your neighborhood veterinarian right away if you believe your pet is experiencing an allergic reaction.

Allergies in pets

Pets may experience allergic reactions to different flora, pollen, and insects, just like people do. The symptoms of hay fever, such as watery, itchy eyes, sneezing, congestion, and sore throats, can be brought on by these allergies. Additionally, they may result in rashes and itchy skin, which may prompt excessive scratching, infection, and hair loss.

Allergies can affect your pet at any stage of their life, so it's important to watch out for any of the symptoms listed above. English Bulldogs and Boston Terriers are two dog breeds that may be more prone to skin allergies.

Ask your veterinarian for help on how to determine the cause of your pet's allergy and manage its symptoms if it occurs.

Finally, make sure your pet has had all recommended vaccinations.

CHAPTER THREE

How can my pets and I benefit from composting

As is well known, composting is a natural process that turns organic waste into a nutrient-rich soil supplement. After that, we may use this as mulch in our garden to assist the soil retain moisture while it is being rebuilt. If we understand how to manage it all well, compost may also be used to make potting soil and clean up after dogs. Additionally, just by doing their part, our furry buddies can contribute...

Knowing exactly what pet waste is the first step towards composting it. As dumb as that may sound. The byproduct of your pet's biological processes is pet waste—what goes in, must come out! Whether it's in the neighborhood park, at home, or on the verge. Pet waste is a catch-all term that covers anything from guinea pig and rabbit droppings to cat litter and canine poop.

Pet waste can be carefully incorporated into your garden as it is a powerful fertilizer.

Pet waste is poisonous to landfills and should never be placed in conventional trash cans due to the presence of harmful bacteria. Although it is a fantastic resource for your garden, it must be composted properly to reduce the possibility of diseases like salmonella and E. coli damaging us. By reintroducing organic material into the ecosystem as a powerful fertilizer and preventing dangerous pollutants from entering rivers through runoff, composting pet waste lowers methane emissions!

It's important to be aware that certain parasites found in feces might spread disease if they enter the food chain through inappropriately managed compost piles or even merely by handling raw meat without washing your hands afterward.

Making pet compost

Avoid going near kid-friendly play areas. Little children have a habit of putting everything in their mouths, and while many substances do aid in immunity building, some are best avoided.

Make sure that piles are kept away from places with food and edible plants when composting at home. Additionally, it is essential to compost pet waste away from locations where kids play. We also need to make sure that our animal companions aren't dispersing it on a whim or digging it up again.

While there are numerous methods for composting pet waste, the simplest is to use a specialized system and handle it similarly to how compost is typically handled within the aforementioned guidelines. Both above and below ground systems are first-rate. Whatever works is always my philosophy! which is constantly evolving. More than anything, gardening is an observational process where you make adjustments as you go.

Since I personally reside on rock and clay hardpan, I utilize above-ground containers. I've experimented with a few various strategies, such using a tumbler. Looking back, I would advise against tumbling pet waste since rotating spreads airborne infections. Wheelie bins can be modified using homemade air filtration [nothing a hole saw and 50mm PVC pipe as mesh-capped extractors can't handle!] to allow for more aerobic activity and set them in the sun for solar acceleration. Usually, I wait a full year for it to ferment before redistributing. If you have the room and no close neighbors, this is fantastic. It all relies on what works best in the given circumstance. While everyone of us has unique needs and spaces, we all want to avoid squandering precious resources or worsening the effects on the environment.

Systems for the ground, such the EnsoPet, are odorless and highly efficient. Additionally, they are very subtle and have very little visual impact in a garden setting. With the exception of the first installation, which calls for the digging of a hole, they are hassle-free and may be installed anywhere that is not within a meter of native trees and food plants. Out of sight and out of memory.

With the exception of pooper scooper time. Works great for both dogs and cats! When the microbes work to break everything down and gradually release into the surrounding soil, using an enzyme accelerant speeds up the process.

Dangerous Dog Digging and Chewing

When you return home, your rose bushes have been dug up and scattered all over the yard, or your slippers have been eaten to pieces. Although your initial reaction could be that your dog is punishing you for leaving them alone at home all day, dogs don't behave in this way out of retaliation or spite. Dogs do, however, discover ways to pass the time when they don't have toys or other people to play with, so it's crucial to provide them lots of acceptable entertainment options before they come up with their own.

Destructive habits typically arise because a dog is bored, lonely, or both. This is the case with many undesired canine behaviors. Expecting your dog, especially a working breed, to sit quietly for extended periods of time as they wait for you to return is neither reasonable nor fair. Dogs are inquisitive and sentient animals by nature. Make sure your dog has adequate mental and physical stimulation to reduce the urge to chew and burrow.

<u>Prevention</u>

Digging

- Keep your dog occupied by giving him lots of engaging toys and changing them out frequently.
- Create a puzzle; When your dog is ready to play, stuff a Kong with peanut butter and freeze it for a few hours and let your dog go at it.
- Give dogs enough cover from the sun and wind, as they frequently dig holes for that purpose (finding a cool nice place to stay).
- Retain your dog inside. (This is your best strategy, if you don't have a sandbox inside your house.)

Chewing

- Assist them in succeeding. If you're having a sock chewer, make sure you don't leave any around the house. They are unable to distinguish between the pricey ski socks you purchased last night and the worn-out, hole-filled pair your children outgrew.
- Make sure your dog always has a variety of chew toys to select from by leaving plenty of acceptable toys around.
- Maintain your dog's physical and mental stimulation. Unwanted behavior can be prevented with frozen Kongs, treat treasure

hunts (which involve "hiding" rewards about the house), lots of playtime, and regular exercise.

The majority of harmful behavior stems from boredom. Enough mental and physical stimulation combined with lots of your attention can keep your dog happy, satisfied, and less likely to dig or chew.

Management

Digging

- Make sure your dog gets lots of attention. Hire a dog walker or think about dog daycare if you will be gone for longer than a few hours at a time.
- Let your dog go. Make sure they have daily walks, play fetch with them, teach them to catch a Frisbee. The majority of dogs need a lot of activity, and when they don't receive enough, they feel restless or nervous.
- Think about harnessing your dog's digging instincts. Give them a small section of the yard (away from the rose bushes) where they are free to dig as much as they want; this will serve as their "legal" digging area. Cover the space with sand or dirt and hide snacks and toys there to tempt them to begin digging. As soon as you discover them mining in a "illegal" region, stop them, direct them

to the proper location, and give them credit for their appropriate digging.

- If at all feasible, keep your dog out of places where they like to dig, or at the very least, make those locations as uninviting as you can.

Chewing

- If you see your dog gnawing on something inappropriate, stop them with a strong "Uh-uh!" and remove the item. As soon as they start chewing on it, replace it with a suitable toy and give them praise.
- Teach your dog to "leave it." This is a useful training technique that you can use to get them to back off of newly painted park benches and chocolate bars on coffee tables, in addition to asking them to leave your slippers alone.
- Take into consideration misting the object of your desire with a non-toxic spray that has a scent that repels dogs.

Pet Interaction in the Garden

Introducing your pets into the garden is more than just letting them run about; it's about establishing a setting where you can enjoy them together and that honors their natural tendencies. Here, we'll look at how to involve your pets in the garden and create a safe space for them to run around, explore, and enjoy the great outdoors.

Comprehending the Behavior of Pets

Recognizing your pet's habits is crucial before embarking on designing a pet-friendly garden. While cats can choose to lounge and climb, dogs might enjoy running and digging. Make sure that your garden is designed to support these innate tendencies and that the surroundings promote good conduct.

Secure and Energizing Plants

Add visually stimulating plants to your pet's environment. For example, cats can enjoy catnip, and dogs may be drawn to particular herbs like lavender or mint. Make sure your pets can safely sniff or eat these plants without risk. It all comes down to designing a setting that engages your pets' senses.

Play Spaces and Playthings

Identifying Areas for Pet-Friendly Play: Set aside designated play spaces for your pets to run around in your garden. Set aside areas that accommodate your pet's playful habits, such as a sandy spot for digging or a patch of grass for a game of fetch. You can save vulnerable plants in other areas of the garden by limiting play activities to designated zones.

Selecting Toys Safe for Pets: Invest on pet-safe outdoor playthings that are made to last. You may amuse and interest your pets with interactive puzzle toys, chew toys made of rubber, or rubber balls. Steer clear of toys that can easily be chewed into little bits that can cause a choking hazard. These toys transform from simple playthings into useful tools for encouraging and increasing your pet's energy.

Factors to lookout for in a Pet-Friendly garden

Cozy Places to Relax

There should be comfortable areas for your pets to unwind in a pet-friendly landscape. Think about putting cozy pillows or beds suitable for pets in shady spots. Dogs could choose a shady area beneath a tree, but cats might prefer high platforms or snug niches. Your pets can relax and take in the surroundings at these resting places.

Water Features for Play and Hydration

Include water elements in your landscape that are pet-friendly. A little pond or shallow birdbath can be used for both entertaining and giving your dogs access to water. Splashing around is fun for many pets, especially on warmer days. Just make sure the water is fresh and clean on a frequent basis.

Protection and Shade

Include pet-friendly shelters or shaded spaces to shield your animals from the sun and unexpected downpours. Pergolas, doghouses, and even well-positioned garden furniture can function as safe havens. By providing shade, you can make sure that your pets may enjoy the garden all day long.

Ground Cover That's Safe for Pets

Select a ground cover that is easy on the paws of your pet. Pet-friendly turf, soft mulch, and grass are all great choices. Steer clear of uncomfortable things like rough stones or thorny bushes. The idea is to have a garden floor that allows your pets to walk around freely and without feeling uncomfortable.

Essentially, the process of designing a garden that is pet-friendly involves balancing the requirements of your plants with the inclinations and tastes of your pets. It's an area where exploration, play, and leisure all coexist together. You're not simply creating a garden; you're creating a real haven that you and your pets can enjoy.

CONCLUSION

Encouraging everyone in the family to enjoy our gardens has several advantages. Our animal companions share our wants and much more. Furthermore, they typically don't roam where we are free to come and leave whenever we like. This gives us even more motivation to design amazing places that offer safe, engaging environments for both of us. while responsibly handling the objects we don't want in our path.

As you reach the final chapters of "Pet-Friendly Gardens," we hope you've found inspiration and practical insights to turn your outdoor space into a flourishing space for both your plants and pets. The beauty of a garden lies not just in its visual appeal but in the shared moments of joy it creates between you and your furry friends.

You've started a life-changing adventure by adopting the pet-friendly gardening techniques covered in this book. Your garden can now be more than a simple collection of plants, it should be a living ecosystem where pets' lively energy, safety, and beauty all coexist peacefully.

We value your opinions much and would be grateful if you could spend a few minutes writing an Amazon review. Your wisdom can help and motivate other pet owners and gardeners on their own life-changing paths.

Your review is more than just a remark; it's an addition to a group of people who are enthusiastic about creating an environment in which plants and pets coexist. Let's weave a fabric of common experiences that speaks to the happiness and contentment that come with pet-friendly gardening.

Thank you for choosing "Introduction Pet-Friendly Gardening" to accompany you on this rewarding journey. I hope your garden keeps growing and that your pets never tire of exploring their colorful outdoor haven. Cheers to your successful gardening!

Printed in Great Britain
by Amazon

48821288R00036